MARTIN COOK

MEDIEVAL BRIDGES

SHIRE ARCHAEOLOGY

Cover illustrations
(Top) Monnow bridge, Monmouth.
(Below left) St Ives bridge, Cambridgeshire.
(Below right) Postbridge clapper bridge, Devon.

I would like to dedicate this book to my mother and late father who were very understanding when I gave up a career in civil engineering to be an archaeologist.

British Library Cataloguing in Publication Data:
Cook, Martin
Medieval bridges. – (Shire archaeology; no. 77)
1. Bridges – History
I. Title
624.2'0902
ISBN 0 7478 0384 6

Published by
SHIRE PUBLICATIONS LTD
Cromwell House, Church Street, Princes Risborough,
Buckinghamshire HP27 9AA, UK.

Series Editor: James Dyer.

ISBN 0 7478 0384 6.

First published 1998.

Printed in Great Britain by
CIT Printing Services Ltd, Press Buildings,
Merlins Bridge, Haverfordwest, Pembrokeshire SA61 1XF.

Contents

Acknowledgements

The author would like to thank Angela Simco and Peter McKeague for introducing him to historic bridges and for their contributions, in one way or another, to this volume. The Sites and Monuments Records, and their staff, of the counties of England all provided valuable information without which this book could not have been written. Angela Simco and Rachel Tedd commented upon the draft text and Steve Rigby drew Figures 7 and 34. Any errors of omission or commission remain the responsibility of the author.

List of illustrations

1
The cultural, historical and economic background

Bridges feature prominently as metaphors in literature, mythology and poetry where good and evil, life and death, civilisation and barbarism, and sanity and madness are juxtaposed. In *The Mayor of Casterbridge* Thomas Hardy describes a bridge used by some inhabitants of the town as a vehicle for escaping the trials of an unjust world. Robert Burns, in *Tam o'Shanter*, portrays the Brig o' Doon as a path to safety from mischief or evil, and in Macaulay's *Horatius* the Pons Sublicius (a bridge across the Tiber in Rome) is a physical link between safety and disaster – a link that must be severed if the city of Rome is to be saved from the Etruscan host. In the novel by Iain Banks the eponymous bridge is used simultaneously as a metaphor for a place between the worlds of life and death, of the conscious and the unconscious and of waking and dreaming.

In the early days of civilisation and commerce a river crossing was often a recognised place of exchange and trade. Bridges were places on which roads converged and were points of contact between communities or areas. Facilities, such as accommodation for travellers, often developed at the head of a bridge, and it is no accident that many public houses or inns are situated by, or take their name from, bridges. The point closest to the mouth of a navigable river where a bridge could be built and an inland port established often resulted in the foundation of a town. The site of London is one of the best-known examples of this phenomenon and has been an urban centre since Roman times.

Precursors of the bridge

The bridge has not always been a common, or even a necessary, part of the English landscape. During periods of history when there was only limited movement of people or goods, the occasional necessity of using a ford or a ferry would not have been seen as a serious inconvenience. Generally speaking, rivers in many areas of England, if left in their natural state, are fordable at various points (figure 1). This was true even of the Medway and the Thames in pre-Roman times, as the account of the Claudian invasion in AD 43 demonstrates. Celtic or German auxiliary troops, attached to the Roman legions, appear to have had little difficulty in fording these rivers and attacking the Britons during the Roman advance. Few Cornish rivers are large or deep enough to lack easy fords, and it is probable that there were no bridges west of

1. A ford at Fartherford, Devon. The crossing points of many small rivers and streams may once have looked like this.

the Tamar in very early times.

Place names can often give a clue to the location of former fords. 'Twyford' suggests that there were two fording places in the same locality. 'Bradford' indicates a broad ford and 'Langford' or 'Longford' a long ford. 'Shalford' represents a shallow ford and 'Stratford', which occurs in various parts of Britain, implies a ford on the line of a Roman street. Often fords remained in use even when a bridge was built. Sometimes the ford was retained because the original bridge was insufficiently wide for certain types of traffic, or as a measure to reduce wear and tear, and thus maintenance costs, on the structure. Fines could be levied against travellers who used the bridge when the ford was passable. On many country bridges, and on the occasional urban one, it is still possible to identify the line of the approach to a former ford. This is usually visible as a broadening of the roadside verge, providing access to the river, either up- or downstream of the bridge (figure 2).

The ford was a common feature of the English landscape until the first half of the twentieth century. The mass production of concrete

2. The approach to a former ford at Spaldwick bridge, Cambridgeshire. The widening of the roadside verge is a good indicator of the presence of a former ford.

pipes, which made culverts easy to construct, and the passing of various pieces of legislation regarding the works that local authorities could undertake, brought about its demise on public and private roads alike. In the nineteenth century it was generally considered that the depth of fording for foot passengers should not exceed three feet, with an extra foot permitted for horse riders. In areas of the former British Empire it was not unusual for travellers to report fords as being 'breast high'. A usual precaution was for travellers to carry a staff with which to test the depth of the water and to provide reassuring support. Hermits and holy men would often station themselves at fords to assist those whose strength or stature was inadequate for the crossing. The most famous of these is traditionally St Christopher. The story of how he carried a mysterious child, who became heavier as the saint progressed and who subsequently revealed himself to Christopher – the 'Christ-bearer' – as Christ himself, is well known.

Small ferries were another common method of crossing a river or stream in early times. Documentary evidence suggests that medieval bridges were so often unsafe and so commonly left in disrepair that a ferry may have been regarded as safer and more reliable. The right to operate a ferry and to retain the income from it was frequently one of the many manorial monopolies, the tolls collected being an additional source of manorial income. The obligation to maintain a bridge was apparently considered so onerous, and the potential income from providing a ferry service so attractive, that a derelict bridge may have been regarded as a financial opportunity. In 1365 a commission inquiring into the delay in repairing a bridge at Newenden, on the border between Kent and Sussex, found an apparent reason in the 'singular profit of the lords of the boat'.

Cable ferries, where a rope or chain is stretched across the river and used by a ferryman to haul a boat or punt across, were in common use in Britain until the nineteenth century. The ferryboat was usually a flat-bottomed sturdily built rectangular vessel, drawing about 450 mm (18 inches) of water when fully loaded and with 250 or 300 mm (10 or 12 inches) of freeboard. A ferry of this kind may still be seen in regular use at Evesham in Worcestershire (figure 3).

3. Hampton ferry at Evesham, Worcestershire.

4.1. Principal Roman towns, roads and known bridges.

The Roman, Saxon and Norman legacy

In Roman times (AD *c*.43 to *c*.410) bridges across anything but the smallest streams were primarily for strategic military purposes, as were the roads that crossed them. Their use by the imperial authorities and others as the means by which a conquered province could be economically exploited was an important but secondary function. Traders and merchants, however, undoubtedly took advantage of the improved communications network when coastal and riverine systems were insufficient to enable them to reach certain destinations.

No complete or even substantially complete Roman bridge survives in England although the remains of many have been recorded (figure 4.1). These are generally small structures on timber piled foundations over minor streams. Typical of such a bridge may be the remains found in a gravel quarry at Aldwinkle in Northamptonshire. Here a series of wooden piles, at intervals of approximately 2.4 metres (7 feet 10 inches), carried a road of limestone chippings and gravel. This may have been on the Leicester to Godmanchester road. The bridge may have been built by the military during the first decades of the Roman occupation, and it was rebuilt at least twice, surviving into the third century.

The most famous and, arguably, the most influential Roman bridge was the one over the Thames at Southwark in London. Roman London may have owed its prosperity to the river, but its location may well have been determined by the need for stable ground adjacent to a river crossing. The modern landscape of central London is the product of at least five millennia of accumulated changes. Excavations on the London waterfront suggest that just before the Roman invasion the Thames was very much wider and shallower than now, the northern edge of the river being about 100 metres (over 100 yards) further north than it is today, and that the area in the vicinity of the City was composed of mudflats dissected by tidal channels. Only at Southwark could the river be approached on the relatively firmer footing provided by a gravel spur and a series of sandbanks. At the foot of Fish Street Hill, on the north bank, adjacent to modern London Bridge, excavations revealed substantial traces of a timber box structure, presumably a pier base, for an early timber bridge dating to the first century AD.

In the British Isles the only known bridges with stone piers dating to the Roman period are those on the frontier with Scotland and at Piercebridge, County Durham. Both the Hadrianic and the Antonine walls had bridges upon them, to carry the wall, a wall-walk or the roads that went with the frontier. Near the fort of Chesters on Hadrian's Wall at least two phases of bridge are known to have carried the frontier across the Tyne. The original Wall Bridge, dating to the Hadrianic period, was replaced by a road bridge in the mid to late second century AD. This seems to have remained in use at least until the late third or early fourth century. No arch stones, or voussoirs, have ever been found, and as some stones had grooves for the insertion of timbers, it is probable that both bridges had flat timber roadways. This was a technique also seen at Polmont Burn near Falkirk on the Antonine Wall. Here the wall and the military way were carried over the course of the burn by a wooden roadway set in stone-lined channels.

The evidence for bridges during the Dark Ages (*c*.410 to *c*.1066) is at best fragmentary. Bridges constructed under the Roman administration must have continued to be used, as some appear to have been repaired. For example, at Staines, in Surrey (formerly in Middlesex), Roman bridge foundations were found next to a late Saxon wooden revetment which may have served as an abutment for a Saxon bridge. There is also clear evidence from Tamworth that bridge building was not a lost art. Excavations on the south side of Lichfield Street revealed an abutment for a tenth-century timber bridge, presumably associated with the construction of the defended town or *burh* ('borough').

Although London appears to have retained its importance as one of the major centres of England during this period, it is uncertain whether there was a bridge across the Thames at this time. A charter of 672-4, which was issued by Frithuwald and Wulfhere in favour of Chertsey Abbey, relating to an area of land near the site of the Roman bridge, does not mention such a structure. This may be significant, as a bridge would have provided a far more conspicuous and definitive landmark than those actually used in the charter. Before the reign of Alfred (871-99), the Thames was, with brief exceptions, a political frontier, and this may have inhibited the establishment of permanent communications across it.

However, at a council held by Alfred in Chelsea in 898 or 899 it appears that matters relating to the security of the area now known as Southwark were discussed. The existence of any defensive works in the vicinity of Southwark at this time would imply that there was a bridge across the river. It is at least possible that by the early eleventh century there existed at London a substantial settlement on both banks of the river, linked by a bridge. A Norse saga (*St Olaf's Saga*), reputedly of this time (but not written down until the thirteenth century), describes 'such a broad bridge across the river that wagons could pass each other on it. On the bridge were bulwarks which reached higher than the middle of a man'. The same saga describes eleventh century Southwark as 'a large trading town'. Other bridges are known in the vicinity of London dating to this period. For example, under the east side of Ludgate Circus an excavation along the east side of the river Fleet found substantial Saxo-Norman timbers which formed the east abutment of a bridge over the Fleet.

Bridges are thought to have existed as part of the defensive arrangements at several *burhs*. At Wallingford it has been suggested that the modern boundary of the borough, on the east bank of the Thames, indicates the previous position of a Saxon bridge head, which was designed to control and block the river. At Barnstaple some compromises had to be reached. The bridge was located outside the defended area of the *burh* at the point on the river that combined both proximity to the town and the shortest distance to the higher ground on the south side of the river. Around the coastline of southern England and the Thames valley in the late ninth and early tenth centuries, it is thought that Edward the Elder created a series of fortresses. These lay on all the major rivers, and many included bridges, in strategic positions, to block access by the Vikings.

After the Norman invasion in 1066 it is likely that traffic of all kinds increased, owing to the more unified control over England and the more peaceful conditions. An entry in the Anglo-Saxon Chronicle, for 1097, states that the bridge at London was in great danger of collapsing, most probably owing to a violent storm and flooding. The bridge must have been considered to be very important, as it was one of the three projects for which labour service was exacted from far beyond London (others were the wall around the Tower of London and the King's Hall at Westminster). The bridge must have been repaired, as by 1176 records state that a wooden bridge, presumably the one referred to in the late eleventh century, was once again almost beyond repair.

Developments during the early medieval period were to change the face of England forever. By the thirteenth century a commercial ethos, common to the whole of western Europe, was developing. It was reflected in the rise of trade in England at this time. In agriculture, production for the market was increasing at the expense of subsistence farming. At a time when commerce was fitful and scanty, fairs and markets afforded opportunities that emergent towns at the gates of castles, cathedrals and monasteries were not yet in a position to provide.

The export trade in wool, which expanded rapidly in the twelfth and thirteenth centuries, is one example of this change. Great nobles and ecclesiastical corporations built up large commercial enterprises at this time, also dealing in leather, corn and smaller sales of utilitarian items such as hurdles. Side-by-side with the expansion of foreign trade was the growth of trade between the developing towns and the surrounding countryside.

Much of this trade had to be conducted overland. Rates used by sheriffs to calculate the recompense due for provisioning fourteenth-century armies suggest that the average price for land haulage was about 1.5d (approximately 0.5p) per ton per mile. The cheapest rate was obtained when four horses were employed to pull a cart loaded with 4 quarters (32 bushels or 1165 litres) of grain. An individual packhorse could be expected to carry 4 bushels (146 litres) of grain, suggesting that carts doubled the carrying capacity of a horse. Therefore packhorses were probably used only in adverse circumstances. The distance that could be covered in a day varied according to the topography and the time of the year. Distances covered by carts varied between 10 and 31 miles (16 and 50 km) a day.

Transport by water was considerably cheaper. Riverine transport was commonly by a batellus or barge. These could carry about 50 quarters of grain at an average cost of about 0.7d (approximately 0.3p) per ton per mile. Sea transport was cheaper still at around 0.2d (approximately 0.1p) per ton per mile. These rates suggest that while land transport was expensive, compared to river or sea transport, it was cheap enough not to have been an insurmountable obstacle to the development of trade.

So, at a time when land transport was comparatively expensive, the provision of a convenient river crossing might have been one of the most cost-effective improvements that could be made to a route. High water levels might have resulted in considerable delay until a ford again became passable, or alternatively, a considerable detour might have been necessary to reach a convenient crossing point. The slower the means of transport, the more time and money a bridge would save.

The means of financing and maintaining medieval bridges

The cost of building a major bridge was a considerable burden in the medieval period. Accumulating funds was a protracted process, tied to the slow rate of turnover, at a time when an enormous proportion of the economy was concerned with agricultural products. The lending of money for profit, or usury, was forbidden by Biblical edict (Leviticus 25, verse 37), legislation and public opinion. Works that required the temporary concentration of considerable amounts of capital were difficult for private enterprise to undertake. After the monarch, the nobility and the church were major landowners and all three controlled significant businesses involving the movement of goods during this time. Secular responsibilities towards bridges (their construction and repair) were discharged as one of the common obligations of society. In Anglo-Saxon texts there are references to *brycg bot* or *brycg geweorc* ('bridge building' or 'bridge works'). In a charter fabricated at Canterbury late in the tenth century the duty of building and repairing bridges is described as being one of the *trinoda necessitas* (three obligations), the others being military service and the maintenance of fortresses.

Towards the close of the thirteenth century, the piety that had earlier manifested itself in the founding of religious houses was directed elsewhere. Sometimes it led to the foundation of a chantry, which was a mass recited at an altar for the well-being of the founder during his or her lifetime and for the repose of the soul after death. An endowment was made to pay for the maintenance of the priests who carried out the mass and frequently part of this endowment was set aside to provide alms for the poor. Less costly and more frequently favoured was an *obit* (a mass sung on the anniversary of the subject's death). Payments for *obits* were usually made to the parish priest, who was responsible for carrying out the rite, and in most cases he was required to distribute alms to the poor. *Obit* bequests were made in kind as well as money. At Bromley, Margaret White, by her will in 1538, ordained that her *obit* should be kept in the church 'out of the increase of two kine' that she left. She also gave three hives of bees to maintain lights at the altars of All Hallows, Saint Anthony and Saint Sepulchre in the church and directed that bread, cheese and drink should be distributed to four poor parishioners. The church also adopted the practice of granting indulgences (remission from time spent in Purgatory) to those who contributed in a major way to bridge construction and repair. As with *obits*, these could be made in cash or in kind. Indulgences became much more common in the fourteenth century, and no public work was undertaken without one right down to the Reformation.

In the medieval period people believed that bridges were under divine protection. A priestly connection with bridges has been thought to account for the pope's title, Pontifex (meaning 'bridge builder', from the Latin *pons,* 'bridge', and *facere,* 'to make'). More recent opinion suggests that the first element of Pontifex is derived from an old Umbrian word, *puntes*, probably relating to certain religious rites involving sacrifices, at a time when it was assumed that the spirit of a stream was malevolent and had to be placated by offerings. The Pontifex was therefore 'the maker of sacrifices'. In the fourth century AD the Christian bishops of Rome took over this title, which is still borne by the pope.

Once a bridge had been built, a grant of 'pontage', the right to exact tolls on people passing over or under the bridge, was likely to be a source of revenue for its maintenance. If a bridge was reported to be in a dangerous condition, an inquiry or inquisition was held to determine who was responsible for its repair. Pontages were only granted when it was found that no person, persons or organisation could be held responsible for the repairs to a bridge. This was always the case when the bridge had been built originally by means of alms or as an act of charity. Such works were instituted without provision for maintenance and, while according to some authorities the donor of a bridge was bound to keep it in repair, this liability did not apparently extend to his heirs, unless they were landowners whose purposes were obviously served by the bridge in question.

It was also common for bridges to be mentioned in wills or bequests. The sums involved were often quite small and often represented acts of piety by the less wealthy members of society. Sometimes the donation would be in kind and might take the form of a pig or a ewe. In 1507 Goditha Wodyll left two measures of barley towards the repair of Tymsill Bridge in Bedfordshire.

4.2. Bridges of the thirteenth century.

The Reformation in England, which began in 1539, brought an end to indulgences, which were abolished with other 'superstitious uses'. Bridges lost their religious character, and chapels, which were frequently built on or adjacent to medieval bridges, were turned over to secular use or demolished (see chapter 3).

The development of trade and the medieval bridge

Trade between Britain and continental Europe was well established even in the pre-Roman Iron Age. When Britain became a Roman province large numbers of small market centres at intervals of 6 to 10

4.3. Bridges of the fourteenth century.

miles (10 to 16 km) were established, both to supply the developing towns and to facilitate the export of goods.

These market centres and the trade networks that they supported declined with the collapse of the Roman system of administration and government during the early fifth century. It was not until the establishment of the Danelaw after the battle of Ethandun in AD 878 that the re-emergence of a market system comparable to that of Roman

4.4. Bridges of the fifteenth century.
Bridges in figure 4 have been obtained from County Sites and Monuments Records and are those that are both adequately dated and located.

times began.

The medieval period has been portrayed as a time of economic self-sufficiency, but the existence of substantial towns such as London, York and Southampton during the medieval period suggests that medieval trade could not have been insignificant. The rapid growth of international trade (in, for example, textiles and pottery) is reflected by the growth in the numbers of bridges after around 1270.

A primary source of information for identifying trade routes during the medieval period are artefacts recovered from archaeological excavations. However, this information is often restricted to the source and ultimate destination of the trade network. Moreover, it will be many years before sufficient excavations have been undertaken to fill in the finer detail of trade networks. In addition, knowledge of the trade in perishable items is unlikely to be addressed in any significant way by these methods.

The systematic study of medieval bridges may offer a way of identifying lost trade routes. For this to be possible, reliably dated and located examples are needed. Surviving bridges are notoriously difficult to date, and ones known only from documentary sources are frequently inadequately located. In addition, surviving documentary sources may refer to a bridge only when it was first constructed in stone, any earlier wooden structure being ignored. Nevertheless, a preliminary distribution of adequately dated and located thirteenth- to fifteenth-century bridges (figures 4.2, 4.3 and 4.4), based solely upon information derived from county Sites and Monuments Records, has some points of interest. Even at this crude level of analysis it is possible to identify developing concentrations of bridges around the ports of London, Bristol and Southampton. Much more work will be needed, both in the field and in documentary sources, and the results will have to be integrated with available archaeological and other documentary information, before a true picture of medieval trade in England can emerge.

2
The mason and bridge design in the medieval period

The medieval mason

Of the few records that survive of medieval building operations, most are of monastic origin. These often comprise adulatory remarks about the building and its instigator but say little or nothing about those who designed and built it. Construction work was a complicated activity, sometimes involving the coordination of large numbers of men, materials and techniques over a lengthy period of time. Men trained in philosophy, religion and politics, who dominated the written word during this era, may have had little understanding of these matters. What they did not understand they either ignored or belittled, and civil work beyond ecclesiastical boundaries is scarcely mentioned at all in written sources. The responsibility for the procurement of labour and materials and the design and construction of stone buildings during the medieval period fell to the master mason who fulfilled the role of both architect and builder.

In the Middle Ages most small towns would have had only one stone building, the church, and only the larger towns and cities had other substantial masonry buildings and circuit walls. The number of masons for whom regular employment could be found in one locality would have been very small. In York the register of Freemen of the City shows that 147 masons were admitted between 1301 and 1558, or about one every two years. Extensive travel in search of work must have been a feature of the mason's life. While some masons became independent building contractors and a few became 'masters of works', the great majority must have remained journeymen all their lives.

The effect of this was that although masons' guilds had a great deal in common with all trade guilds, they were not tied to particular places. The paucity of references to municipal guilds of masons in the fourteenth and fifteenth centuries suggests that local guilds of masons were not strongly developed in the boroughs before the days of sixteenth-century Elizabethan labour legislation. This was also reflected in the statutes relating to the practice of the mason's trade, which permitted masons to follow their craft in any town, whether 'free' of it or not, so long as they were 'free' of some given town or city. This is one explanation for the appellation 'freemason', although it is possible that the word is derived from the carving of freestone (stone that could be cut easily in any direction). The mobility of masons at this time was reflected in the masons' lodge, the unique feature of which was its impermanence.

Craftsmen who were continually on the move could not take advantage of a permanent guild, and the mason's life centred upon the lodge or workshop where he was temporarily employed. For smaller or short-lived projects this may have been little more than a large tent providing shelter and basic accommodation. However, in the larger towns or cities such as York, where there were stone structures requiring constant work or repair, a masons' yard would be established with a more substantial lodge or workshop. In York the lodge attached to the minster was originally intended to accommodate twenty masons but was rebuilt in 1412 for twelve.

Masons were frequently consulted as experts in the provision or purchase of stone and were sent to quarries to inspect the material; on occasion they also worked in quarries themselves. The Caernarvon Castle building account of 1316-17 shows that a dozen 'layers' (*cubitores*) worked as scapplers (people who roughly shaped the stone) in the quarry at Aberpwll and that three masons (*cementarii*) worked there as cutters in April 1317. There is very little evidence for mason apprentices before the end of the fourteenth century, and it is likely that an oral tradition was followed in the training of novices. It may be that the quarries provided initial training in preparing stone, from which a trainee might progress into the ranks of rough masons and ultimately

5. Detail of Mordiford bridge, Herefordshire, showing corbels.

become a stonecutter or hewer.

Medieval quarries seem on the whole to have been small, located as close to the proposed work as possible, although stone for important buildings or for the dressings of lesser structures might be brought from farther afield. The quarries in the Isle of Purbeck were particularly favoured, and many churches built between 1170 and 1350 incorporated Purbeck marble. Quarries were acquired by gift, purchase and – sometimes – by lease.

Three methods for working a quarry were commonly employed. These were: for those responsible for the erection of a particular building to open up and work the quarry; for quarrymasters to work the quarry and sell the stone to those engaged in construction work; or for quarrymasters to work the quarries and, in the capacity of mason-contractors, to use the stone from their own quarries to erect buildings by contract. As the rise of the mason-contractor was a relatively late development in the English building industry, instances of quarrymen acting as mason–contractors in the Middle Ages are not very common.

Engineering theory and practice in the medieval period

Until about 1270 the only known substantial work on the theory of construction had come down from Roman times: that of Vitruvius. The evidence is limited, but it is likely that the earliest medieval bridges were built in the Roman style with stone piers and a wooden deck. A very few bridges may to this day carry vestigial traces of this early form of construction. Beneath one arch of the bridge at Mordiford, near Hereford (figure 5), corbels project just beneath the springing of the

6. The principal parts of a bridge.

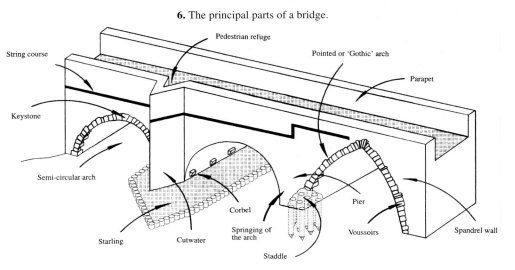

String course

Keystone

Semi-circular arch

Starling Cutwater Springing of the arch Corbel Staddle Voussoirs Pier

Pedestrian refuge

Pointed or 'Gothic' arch

Parapet

Spandrel wall

7. A reconstruction of Mordiford bridge, Herefordshire, as it might have been in the early medieval period.

existing stone arches. These corbels may once have carried wooden beams supporting a wooden carriageway between the stone piers (figure 7). An alternative explanation is that they were intended to be used as temporary supports for timbers supporting the stone arch during its construction. In most such cases the latter explanation is the most likely. However, at Mordiford excavations over this arch, preparatory to repairs, revealed a former road surface that was too low to pass conveniently over the arch now present.

Early medieval bridges were frequently quite narrow. Until the twentieth century most traffic consisted of horse-drawn vehicles, and before about 1750 the volume of such traffic was so small that two carts would rarely meet on a bridge. Even if they did, the risk of an accident was negligible. In the early Middle Ages in Ireland, in France and probably in England too, most bridges had no stone parapets. Documentary evidence relating to Rochester bridge suggests that it was unsafe to cross it on horseback or in high winds, and the death of William Ferrers in 1254 on St Neots bridge in Cambridgeshire has been attributed to the lack of any form of barrier. However, it is known from nineteenth-century evidence that some bridges, such as that at Harrold in Bedfordshire (figure 8), had wooden railings supported by wooden cantilevers set in the body of the bridge. The cut-off remains of these cantilevers survive on the downstream elevation, immediately below the modern road level. Bridges that retain a timber railing are now rare. A fairly modern example, dating to the early nineteenth century, is Oakley South bridge in Bedfordshire (figure 9). It is possible that the

8. Harrold bridge, Bedfordshire.

9. Oakley South bridge, Bedfordshire: an unusual bridge with railings.

omission of stone parapets was owing not to lack of funds but to two other factors. Firstly, wooden railings were the traditional method of fencing a bridge with a wooden roadway, and this tradition may have been continued when stone arches became the usual form of construction. Secondly, it seems to have been appreciated that a narrow bridge with parapet walls was more likely to be washed away in severe floods than a similar bridge with no parapets or only a railing.

The semicircular arch, characteristic of Roman construction in continental Europe, was also favoured by masons in Britain at the beginning of the later medieval period. These arches were barrel vaults which exerted pressure evenly along the whole length of their springing. These required extensive support during construction, as the arch did not become self-supporting until it was complete. If the supports were removed too early the arch could collapse. If removal of the supports was delayed beyond the point when the completed arch had settled, their subsequent removal could prove very difficult.

The ribbed arch, so characteristic of medieval bridges (figure 10), was introduced first as a technical innovation into the churches of the late twelfth and thirteenth centuries. Serious weaknesses can arise in barrel vaults if they are required to be pierced for windows or cross-

10. Yeolmbridge bridge, Cornwall, showing ribbed arch.

passages, and in churches the principal advantage of a ribbed vault was that it could be open in more than one direction without suffering any loss of strength. In such a vault the ribs are self-supporting, the thrust being transferred along the line of the ribs, enabling the spaces in between to be filled or left open as required. Since the arch of a bridge is required to be open in one direction only, the primary advantages of a ribbed vault in bridge construction were somewhat different. Since the ribs were self-supporting, less temporary timberwork, or centring, was needed during construction. A further effect of ribbed construction was that the volume of stone to be cut accurately was about one third of that needed if the full width of the bridge were to be constructed in such stone. This may have been an important consideration for some bridges where the skill to undertake such work was at a premium or suitable stone was in limited supply. In addition, the weight of the masonry in the arch, and thus the lateral thrust on the piers, was reduced. There is also the philosophical dimension of construction in the medieval period to be considered. The design of a structure was as much the preserve of the philosopher as of the architect or mason, and much was discussed and written about the philosophically 'correct' form of building. Therefore,

11. Kirkby Lonsdale bridge, Cumbria, showing chamfered voussoirs and three orders of arch ring.

12. Exeter bridge, Devon, showing alternate voussoirs in different coloured stone.

13. The packhorse bridge at Utterby, Lincolnshire. Even this tiny bridge was constructed with a ribbed arch.

the adoption of ribbing in medieval bridges may have had as much to do with aesthetics as structural need. This case is supported by the use of chamfered ribs and multiple orders of arch ring (figure 11), the use of stone of alternating colours, and the superfluous sophistication employed in some bridges (figure 12). Chamfers are valuable in buildings to increase the amount of light that can enter through an opening but have little practical value in a bridge. The value of ribbed arches has been noted above, but in such a small structure as the packhorse bridge at Utterby in Lincolnshire (figure 13) they must have been for appearance only.

In 1485, as the medieval period gave way to the Renaissance, an Italian, Leon Battista Alberti, wrote a treatise on architecture in which he tried to take what he believed to be of value from earlier works in order to establish a new theory of building. He also dealt with bridges and gave advice about different types of stone and how they should be treated before and during construction. He paid particular attention to the best site for the location for a bridge:

> [It ought] to be contrived in a place where it may easily be erected, and without too great an expense, and where it is likely to be the most durable. We should therefore choose a ford where the water is not too deep; where the shore is not too steep; which is not uncertain and movable, but constant and lasting. We should avoid all whirlpools, eddies, gulfs, and the like inconveniences common in bad rivers. We should also most carefully avoid all elbows, where the water takes a turn.

Alberti described the use of what we now know as coffer dams and detailed the construction of the foundations, the piers, arches and roadway. He considered the relative advantages of pointed or semi-circular cutwaters and decided that while either would suffice, a pointed cutwater was to be preferred.

Bridge design in the medieval period

The medieval bridge builder depended to a large extent on finding ground of good bearing capacity at regular intervals across the width of the river, on which the bridge's piers could be founded. If such ground was spaced irregularly then the easiest course was to vary the span of the arches to accommodate the irregularity. With the semicircular arch, variations in the span of adjacent arches would cause them to rise to different heights, resulting in the carriageway not being level. Alternatively, the bearing capacity of the bed of the river could be improved in the vicinity of the pier by the use of staddles. These were closely spaced groups of piles driven into the river bed where a pier was to be located (figure 6). Staddles were attractive to medieval bridge builders because they could be used on all river beds except rock. At Rochester bridge the staddles comprised a large number of iron-tipped wooden piles driven close together into the river bed in the position where the piers were to be built. These were surrounded by starlings –

wedge-shaped constructions that comprised contiguous timber piles driven into the river bed around each pier, the open space within being filled with rubble. The staddles provided a firm bearing on which the piers could be built and the starlings protected the upstream and downstream face of the pier from the effects of scour caused by eddies (figure 34). They also protected the upstream face from collision with floating debris. In the twelfth century a number of major bridges, including Old London Bridge, were constructed in this way.

Towards the end of the twelfth century, pointed, or Gothic, arches were introduced into ecclesiastical buildings. This design of arch allowed the span to be altered without affecting the height of the arch, giving the mason more flexibility in the detailing of the often complex roof vaulting. When combined with the technique of ribbing, it resulted in structures of impressive grace. The pointed arch was the development for which the bridge builders had been waiting. For the first time, at the close of the twelfth century, masons could reconcile the need for variable arch spans with that for constant arch height. Settlement, which was inevitable when inadequate centring was used or when inadequate foundations were constructed, did not unduly distort the visual appearance of a pointed arch or risk causing collapse to the same extent as it did for a semicircular arch. These arches could also provide greater headroom for boats. The disadvantage of the pointed arch was that it required more piers in the river channel, thus restricting the flow.

It was noted in chapter 1 that during the medieval period it was

14. Ludlow bridge, Shropshire, showing massive medieval piers.

difficult to complete major engineering works at one time. This resulted in even fairly small projects being spread out over a number of years, and larger ones over decades. Old London Bridge, begun around 1176, is reputed to have taken 33 years to complete. No arch of a bridge could depend upon its fellows for support: each had to be capable of standing independently until work could recommence. This independent stability was achieved by building massive piers (figure 14), their combined width sometimes occupying half of the river channel.

The starling probably influenced the development of the cutwater. The shape of the starling, when carried up to parapet height, formed refuges (figure 15) for pedestrians on what were frequently narrow carriageways. It has been suggested that these refuges were also intended as platforms from which the rescue of persons washed away from an adjacent ford might be attempted. Early medieval bridges in their original form either had no cutwaters at all or had them on the upstream face only. During the later medieval period cutwaters were introduced on the downstream face of piers, either as part of the original design or as additions to an existing pier. When starlings ceased to be used, the base of the pier no longer had any protection from the effects of scour (see below, chapter 4). This was rectified by setting cobbles or pitched stones in the bed of the stream between the piers, extending some distance up and down stream to form an apron. This had the effect of forcing the river to run in a stone channel in the immediate vicinity of the bridge, protecting the base of the piers.

15. Ludlow bridge, Shropshire, showing a typical pedestrian refuge.

16. The bridge of Hebden Bridge, West Yorkshire, showing an example of a segmental arch.

In the fourteenth century came the development of the segmental arch (figure 16). This, like the semicircular arch, is part of a circle, but it is a smaller part of a larger circle. It combined the advantages of the semicircular arch and the pointed arch: the flatter profile could keep the roadway level, while fewer piers were required in the stream, so that there was less obstruction to navigation and flood waters had a freer passage. In general, medieval masons seem to have discovered the margins of safety through observation and experience, with established pragmatic solutions providing the safest basis for experiment. The segmental arch, however, must have represented a leap both in technology and in faith, since such an arch has profoundly different structural requirements from either a semicircular or a pointed arch. Although it was appreciated that arches generate an element of horizontal thrust, this force was too complex for calculation by fourteenth-century mathematics; on the other hand, there was sufficient empirical knowledge to ensure that it was taken into account in established forms of construction. This, however, was not true of the segmental arch, and we can only admire the intuition and courage of the later medieval builders who adopted it.

The effect of topography on medieval bridges

At a time when technology was in its infancy, topography was a major influence on the style of bridge that was constructed, no matter what its scale.

On wide, flat flood plains, rivers tend to be broad and fairly shallow. Both carriage and packhorse bridges usually consist of several arches and are often narrow and humpbacked (figure 17). There may be a ford alongside and perhaps a causeway leading to the bridge for the benefit of foot passengers, riders or packhorse traffic (figure 18). Such causeways may be of stone or earthen construction, pierced from time to time with

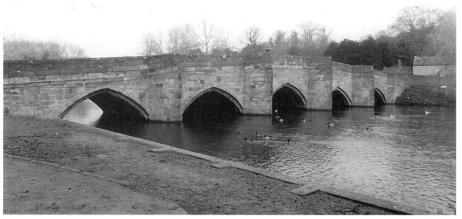

17. Bakewell bridge, Derbyshire. This is the 'humpbacked' form that is typical of bridges on wide flood plains.

18. Harrold bridge, Bedfordshire, showing the foot causeway.

19. Mordiford bridge, Herefordshire. This bridge is built out from the river cliff on the right-hand side of the photograph.

20. Twizel bridge, Northumberland. The grand scale of this bridge was possible because of its situation in a gorge.

small flood-relief arches. More rarely, they may run across a series of land arches. If the river was very shallow and readily fordable for most of the year then a packhorse or clapper-type bridge may have been considered sufficient.

On some flood plains the river, although meandering, has vigorously eroded its bed or banks. This has resulted in either a symmetrical, deeply incised channel or a river cliff on one side of the river and a gently sloping flood plain on the other. The former situation usually produces a bridge with a level carriageway, with several arches carrying it across the river. The latter usually results in a number of small land arches forming an approach causeway across the flood plain before the bridge proper, built out from the river cliff, is reached (figure 19).

Bridges in gorges offered the medieval mason the best opportunity to demonstrate his virtuosity. These were built only when a valley was sufficiently deep to contain the very large arch that was necessary and sufficiently narrow to make such a bridge a feasible proposition (figure 20). A gorge is invariably cut through rock, which provided these bridges with the most stable abutments and foundations possible. However, they were no more typical of medieval bridges than cathedrals were typical of medieval buildings. They should therefore be admired as the height to which medieval engineering could aspire.

3
Other aspects of medieval bridges

Causeways

Medieval causeways appear to have been well-built structures, comparable to the bridges they served in terms of engineering accomplishment, rather than merely being piles of earth thrown up by unskilled labour. Unfortunately, unlike the adjacent bridges (which have usually survived despite centuries of alterations), medieval causeways often lie beneath later works which completely conceal their existence or original form. Alternatively, the route of the modern road may be slightly different from its medieval counterpart, with the result that the original causeway has long since become redundant. In such cases, lack of maintenance has resulted in rapid decay, and stone may have been removed for use in buildings nearby. Information about causeways is therefore patchy.

Causeways were provided to give convenient access to a bridge over the potentially difficult terrain of the flood plain. The sixteenth-century antiquary John Leland gives a striking account of their importance in his description of the bridge at Stratford-upon-Avon:

> Afore the time of Hughe Clopton there was but a poore bridge of timber and no causey to come to it; whereby many poore folkys [and] othar refused to come to Stratford when Avon was up, or coming thithar stoode in jeoperdy of lyfe, . . .

Causeways are not a simple, homogeneous group of structures. They include those intended solely for the pedestrian, those suitable for the passage of horses and those built to accommodate the entire width of the road on its approach to the bridge. Causeways, like medieval bridges, were altered and modified. Examples demonstrate that they were widened and lengthened, and there were no doubt countless minor changes associated with maintenance works throughout their life. With regard to crossing a river they were of equal importance to the bridge they served and should receive the same consideration.

At Barnstaple and other *burhs* such as Plympton, a bridge and causeway formed an integral part of the town defences from the early tenth century. One function of the contemporary Barnstaple bridge was to prevent inland penetration by Viking ships up the river Yeo. Access to it was provided by a long causeway leading to the higher ground around the village of Pilton to the north. It is likely that this causeway is as early as the *burh*, as without it there would have been little point in the north gate being where it was clearly situated.

An extended project of bridge maintenance and repair in Bedfordshire, begun in 1982 and completed during the early 1990s, has provided

21. Harrold bridge, Bedfordshire. The photograph shows one arch of the foot causeway, typical of its kind, where successive widenings have taken place by the use of additional arches between the cutwaters.

much detailed information about medieval causeways. The causeway approaching Harrold bridge (figure 18) is of stone construction, pierced by flood arches at regular intervals and provided with cutwaters on the upstream side. It has been widened on three separate occasions (figure 21) and lengthened at least once. The railing is a modern addition. At Turvey bridge (figure 22), a short length of the original causeway has

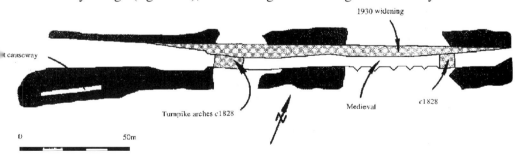

22. Turvey bridge, Bedfordshire. Remains of the medieval causeway lie to the south-west of the bridge and formerly joined it to the east of the turnpike arches.

survived in a thicket at the side of the modern road. Most of this causeway comprised timber beams resting on stone piers, although the surviving length is a narrow but well-built structure of stone (figure 23). Widening of Turvey bridge and extensive widening of what was once a narrow channel running parallel with the main river have made it difficult to relate the remains of the causeway to the original bridge. However, the irregular alignment of the substantially unaltered southern side of the bridge suggests how the causeway and bridge formerly linked up. Finally, at Stafford Bridge near Oakley, documentary evidence indicates that there was a foot causeway. In 1522 Thomas Knight of Bedford left ten shillings '... for the repair of the long causeway beyond Stafford bridge'. This causeway was 1.5 metres (5 feet) wide and up to 380 metres (415 yards) long and appears to have been similar in character to the one at Harrold.

Clapper and packhorse bridges

These are two of the few surviving types of monument associated with the packhorse trade. They were built to protect goods from the damage that might be incurred if a stream was forded – not necessarily a swollen stream, as one reduced to a trickle could prove just as damaging.

23. Turvey bridge, Bedfordshire. A photograph of the remains of the medieval causeway, now lost to view in a thicket beside the modern road.

It is unwise to ride or drive a horse through shallow water. If the animal is sticky and uncomfortable, the desire to roll, rid itself of its load and cool down often becomes irresistible when it finds itself splashing through water. Such an occurrence would have been disastrous for a packhorse train as once one animal had succumbed to temptation it would probably have been imitated by others.

The term 'clapper' is of unknown derivation, although many suggestions about its origin have been made. These include suggested derivations from the Anglo-Saxon words *cleaca* and *clam,* which refer, respectively, to stepping stones and twigs or sticks (perhaps suggesting crude tree-trunk constructions). The term 'clam' is still common in parts of Devon and Cornwall. In Sussex, and also in Berkshire, the word 'clapper' means a plank and is often applied to a raised footway alongside roads subject to flooding.

Nowadays the description 'clapper bridge' is usually applied to the bridges of drystone piers and massive stone slabs typical of the moors of Devon (figure 24). They are, however, also found in other areas of Britain where the local geology is capable of producing large slabs of stone, including North and West Yorkshire and parts of Cumbria and Lancashire.

24. Postbridge clapper bridge, Devon.

The simple construction of these bridges (some are merely a single slab of stone spanning a small stream or rivulet) has led people to overestimate their antiquity. Such basic structures are very difficult to date, but it is now thought that most surviving examples are no earlier than the fourteenth century, and many are known to be considerably later. They are commonly found on known packhorse routes, often adjacent to a ford, and provide an alternative crossing for pedestrians and horses.

Of more sophisticated construction were the packhorse bridges themselves. As a group, these show all the characteristics of the larger medieval bridge, but in miniature. One of the smallest, Utterby packhorse bridge in Lincolnshire (figure 13), even has ribs. Packhorse bridges are easily recognisable, as they are very narrow, frequently allowing passage, even in single file, in only one direction at a time, and have low parapets or even none at all. The lack of parapets is usually explained as having been necessary to accommodate the loads (packs) that were slung on each side of the horse, although the absence of parapets was a common feature of many medieval bridges (see chapter 2). Some examples, such as the packhorse bridge at Sidford in Devon, have been buried within modern construction during road widening schemes.

Few packhorse bridges have been studied in detail but essential repairs to Sutton packhorse bridge in Bedfordshire revealed information that may be typical of such bridges elsewhere. It is about 40 metres (44 yards) long and about 2.3 metres (7 feet 6 inches) wide at its narrowest point over the arches, which were originally pointed. There is a cutwater on the upstream side only, and the bridge lies beside a ford that is still in use today. Settlement of the footings had caused cracks in the east abutment. Excavation of the stream bed revealed four elm beams which were continuous under both abutments and the central pier. These would have been intended to provide a stable foundation on which construction could begin and must have been an original feature of the bridge. Radiocarbon determinations have given a date in the thirteenth century for the felling of the timbers, which showed no signs of reuse. When first built the bridge must have been higher than it is now, as the upper arch ring, near the crown of both arches, has been truncated and a string course added (figure 25). This suggests that Sutton bridge would originally have been humpbacked, with steeper approaches than currently exist. This may have required the provision of long steps in the carriageway such as those visible at Moulton packhorse bridge in Suffolk (figure 26).

Chapels and chantries

In medieval England the only means of travel for most people was by road. Even if the roads of the time were not always as bad as they have

25. Sutton packhorse bridge, Bedfordshire, showing the truncated arch rings.

26. Moulton packhorse bridge, Suffolk.

27. St Ives bridge, Cambridgeshire, showing the chapel on one of the mid-river piers.

sometimes been portrayed, during winter many of them were close to impassable, and there were other dangers. In 1295 Matthew of Dunstable founded the 'chantry of Biddenham Bridge' for the safety of travellers who were in danger from thieves. Some chapels included a very early celebration known as the 'chantry of morrow-mass'. This was sometimes sung at four or five o'clock in the morning to enable travellers to hear a mass before taking to the road.

Bridge chapels were built throughout the Middle Ages. The earliest seem to belong to the twelfth century, for example the chapel of St James at the bridge of Burton-upon-Trent. The chapel on Old London Bridge was originally erected in the thirteenth century, although it was rebuilt in the perpendicular style at the end of the fourteenth. The records of the fourteenth century suggest that it was during this period that the greatest number of bridge chapels was built, including those at Nottingham, Rochester, Huntingdon, Stockport and Bedford. Chapels of the fifteenth century include those at St Ives (figure 27) and Ludlow.

As a rule a chapel was built on or above a starling on one side of the bridge, though sometimes it stood at one end. On London Bridge a two-storey chapel was built within one of the piers. A chapel at Turvey bridge, Bedfordshire, may have been located on an island in the river. The chapel on Droitwich bridge in Worcestershire was probably unique. Leland reported a wooden structure that lay across the bridge, the road

28. Wakefield bridge, West Yorkshire. The chapel is a nineteenth-century reproduction of the original medieval structure.

separating the pulpit from the congregation.

There are surviving records of many chantries in bridge chapels, notably at Wakefield, Rotherham, Rochester and Old London Bridge. The finest remaining bridge chapel in Britain is that at Wakefield, West Yorkshire, on the bridge spanning the Calder (figure 28). This example is mentioned by Leland and, although substantially rebuilt, remains a good example of Decorated Gothic architecture of the mid fourteenth century. A further use of bridge chapels generally is indicated in the Chantry Certificate of 1546. This suggests that they were used in times of plague or other pestilence, to enable the sick to attend divine service, leaving the parish church for the use of the rest of the parishioners.

The end of bridge chapels came in the mid sixteenth century. The survey of monastic property undertaken in 1534 by Henry VIII shows three priests based at the chapel on Wakefield bridge who received £6 each per annum. Following the Chantries Act of 1545 a second survey again showed three priests. In 1547, after the accession of Edward VI, Parliament passed the second Chantries Act, under which all colleges, free chapels and chantries passed to the crown. Altar plate, vestments and other small items were sold off and the buildings were either demolished or turned to other uses.

Defences, gatehouses and lock-ups

In ninth-century France a new role in warfare emerged for bridges. They were fortified and garrisoned to prevent an enemy crossing over or passing under them. Charles the Bald constructed bridges on the Seine to prevent Norse men from moving upriver. In England, bridges were thought to have existed as part of the defensive arrangements at several *burhs*. As described in chapter 1, a series of fortresses or *burhs* are believed to have been associated with bridges, in a systematic attempt to block access by the Viking fleet to all the major rivers and estuaries.

It was during the later Middle Ages that the fortified bridge was extensively developed on the continent. In England, fully fortified bridges were comparatively rare, although many important medieval cities, such as Bedford, Chester and Worcester, had a defensive gateway on or by the bridge. Only two now remain: at Warkworth in Northumberland and the Monnow bridge at Monmouth. At Warkworth there was a plain rectangular gatehouse of which only the ground floor and arch remain. However, at Monmouth survives a late thirteenth-century bridge with a gatehouse added above the pier nearest the town in either the very late thirteenth century or the very early fourteenth (figure 29).

When it was first built, the Monnow Gate was very different from how it is today. The bridge would have been considerably narrower, and pedestrians and vehicles would have passed through the single arched passage in the centre of the tower. The gate would also have been without the three machicolation arches, which would have obstructed the portcullis had they been present. It would, however, have had the cross-shaped arrow slits which remain a prominent feature today. These are typical of the late thirteenth century and were developed from plain loops. The horizontal slits allowed an increased field of view from within.

Town walls and defended gateways provided a benefit beyond the obvious asset of protection. The enclosed area became more attractive as a trading centre, as it could be policed, enabling order to be more easily maintained. Gateways allowed the ingress and egress of merchants and travellers to be monitored and regulated, and they also facilitated the collection of tolls.

When the development of gunpowder made castles, town walls and fortified bridges redundant, the towers or rooms over the gateways were frequently used as prisons. This was the case with the tower on the English Bridge at Shrewsbury. In the reign of Elizabeth I the tower by the Dee bridge at Chester was let, with provision for its repossession in the event of war.

29. The gatehouse on Monnow bridge, Monmouth.

Shops and houses

During the Middle Ages and for a long time afterwards, many urban bridges were covered with houses and shops, the rents from which contributed to the upkeep of the structure. Old Bristol Bridge, over the Avon, had houses upon it. They were an addition to the original four-arched bridge, which was 4.5 metres (15 feet) wide and 50 metres (55 yards) long. To permit their construction, a wall 1.2 metres (4 feet) thick was built on each side of the bridge, parallel to it and about 4.8 to 5.4 metres (16 to 18 feet) from it. It rested on the starlings which projected up and downstream, and it was pierced with arches to match the bridge. Large beams were then laid from the bridge to the parallel wall, and the houses were built upon them. Subsequent modifications included additional beams, cantilevered out beyond the walls and supported by trusses from below, to increase space. Some buildings had cellars in the piers of the bridge.

30. High Bridge, Lincoln.
Note the sixteenth-century
buildings on the bridge.

Trade on or related to bridges was not restricted to shops. Trading centres or markets very often became established at bridgeheads, and even on the bridge itself. During the reign of Edward I, Gilbert Nevil had a market on Thursdays at Glandford Bridge at Brigg in Lincolnshire. He also benefited from tolls levied on all merchandise sold or bought at the market as well as on all carts passing over the bridge. At Leeds, a weekly cloth market was held on the old bridge, until it was moved at the end of Charles II's reign. The cloth was displayed for sale on the parapet, and the clothiers were summoned to assemble by the ringing of a bell in the bridge chapel. Fairs, which were primarily markets during the medieval period, were held on Bishop's Bridge, Norwich amongst others.

The High Bridge at Lincoln (figure 30) has had shops on it since 1391 when John de Sutton is known to have bequeathed 'two Shoppes on the great bridge at Lincoln'. Excluding the buildings on the Pulteney Bridge at Bath, which are merely lock-up shops, and a bridge at Frome, Somerset, which has modern houses upon it, the High Bridge is the only remaining bridge in England which retains this link with the past. The existing half-timbered buildings date from 1540.

Mills

By the late eleventh century watermills were a common feature of the landscape in most parts of England. Domesday Book records somewhere between 5600 and 6100 mills, depending upon how the many references to 'half a mill' or 'one sixth of a mill' are counted. Apart from their presence, the only other information that Domesday records about these mills is their value. It is apparent that a mill's value depended upon two factors: its proximity to a centre of population and the size of watercourse on which it was built. In Huntingdonshire, for example, mills of high and intermediate value were on the rivers Ouse and Nene, while along the smaller rivers were located mills of low value. Except for certain areas, such as Devon and Cornwall which seem to have had relatively few mills before the late eleventh century, little expansion of milling capacity appears to have taken place until the invention of the windmill. This may have been because most suitable locations for a watermill had been taken by this time.

Attempts appear to have been made to improve the characteristics of some rivers to enable additional mills to be constructed. In the thirteenth and early fourteenth centuries navigable rivers were under the jurisdiction of the Lord High Admiral, who was empowered to survey and order the removal of any mills that impeded rivers or injured harbours. The first English law on the subject, apparently dating from the thirteenth century but entered in the *Liber Niger Admiralitatis* ('Black Book of the Admiralty') in about 1360, states:

> Let inquiry be made of all those who maintain on the great streams and channels of havens or ports, weirs, kiddels, blindstakes, watermills or other instruments ... whereby sailors or vessels may commonly be injured.

The Admiralty laws on this subject were subsequently continued by statute (45 Edward III c 2; 1 Henry IV c 12; 12 Edward IV c 7) and remained in force until the middle of the fifteenth century.

The construction of a masonry bridge may have provided an opportunity to establish a mill where previously the flow of the river was inadequate or without falling foul of the navigation laws. As has been noted above, the piers of such a bridge frequently obstructed as much as half of the width of the river. This resulted in the raising of the water level upstream of the bridge. The best-known example is Old

31. The mill at Turvey bridge, Bedfordshire.

London Bridge, where the difference in water level between the upstream and downstream sides was about 1.5 metres (5 feet). With little effort, the cutwaters and piers of a bridge could be incorporated into a mill-race. Sometimes the mill was built on the bridge itself, but more usually it lay on one of the banks. At Lugg bridge, near Hereford, the remains of a stone structure lie on the edge of the river about 150 metres (164 yards) upstream of the bridge. This is thought to have been one of four mills mentioned in Domesday Book for the manor of Lugwardine. It is not known when this mill went out of use, but it may have been when Lugg bridge was first constructed in stone and a new mill erected immediately downstream of it. The construction of the bridge in this form is itself undated, but in 1464 indulgences were granted for the repair of the bridge, perhaps suggesting a date of construction in the late fourteenth century. Mills in Bedfordshire, such as those by Turvey and Bromham bridges (figure 31), favoured a position upstream of the bridge.

4
The medieval bridge in the modern world

Changes in attitudes and the law relating to medieval bridges

Up until the time of Magna Carta (1215) the *trinoda necessitas* required freemen to do labour service to construct or maintain bridges and fortresses and undertake military service as and when required. After 1215 only those who already had an obligation to maintain a bridge would subsequently be required to do so. The Statute of Winchester, in 1285, affirmed that each lord of the manor was responsible for the upkeep of the king's highway, although no specific mention was made of bridges.

The right to grant indulgences, such as that given in 1515 in return for alms and subsidies towards the repair of the bridge and highway at Mordiford on the river Wye, was an important means by which bridges were maintained in the medieval period. The Reformation, at which all the monastic establishments, chantries and the like were dissolved and their funds, lands and buildings confiscated, put an end to this system.

The Dissolution of the monasteries left gaps, such as the care for the poor, hospital work and the reclamation of the fens, which were very tardily filled in most cases. This may have been because the church, in common with other landowners, had already been evading its legal obligations as well as its pious duties towards the traveller. However, steps to provide for the care of bridges had preceded the Reformation (which began in 1539). In 1530-1 the Statute of Bridges stated that:

> ... in many parts of the realm it cannot be known and proved what hundred, tithing, wapentake, city, borough, town or parish, nor what persons certain or body politic ought of right to maintain the bridges.

It was therefore enacted that:

> ... where the responsibility cannot certainly be allocated, the said bridges, if they be without a city or town corporate, shall be made by the inhabitants of the shire or riding in which the said bridge decayed happen to be and if it be within any city or town corporate then by the inhabitants of the city or town corporate.

Justices of the Peace, sitting in Quarter Sessions, were empowered to enquire into bridges broken on the highway 'to the damage of the King's leige people' and, where no landowner could be found liable, were given the power to raise any necessary labour and skills and such money as they thought fit for the repair and maintenance of such bridges.

In 1888 the system of local government called county councils was created and the proceedings formerly undertaken by the Quarter Sessions were transferred to the new councils. However, it was not until the first decades of the twentieth century that all remaining privately maintained bridges on the public highway were transferred to public ownership.

It was in the early 1880s, with the passing of the first Ancient Monuments Act, that ancient and historic bridges were first given legal protection as 'scheduled ancient monuments'. Amendments to this Act were made in 1913 and 1931. In 1947 the original lists of buildings of special architectural or historic interest were produced and some bridges were 'listed'. In 1979 the Ancient Monuments and Archaeological Areas Act was passed, superseding all previous Acts. The lists of historic buildings were themselves revised in 1990 under the Planning (Listed Buildings and Conservation Areas) Act. In cases where a bridge is both listed and scheduled, the scheduled monument legislation takes precedence over the listed building controls.

Structures that are listed may not be altered, extended or demolished without listed building consent. However, if the works are urgently required in the interests of health or safety, or for the preservation of the structure, and when it is not practicable to achieve this by repairs or temporary support or shelter, the work may go ahead. In any event, the works must be limited to the minimum necessary to achieve the purpose. Listed building consent is not required, however, for repairs which will not result in any alteration in appearance or character.

Works may not be carried out on structures that are scheduled without the consent of the Secretary of State for Culture, Media and Sport. If any works are carried out without consent, or the monument is damaged, a criminal offence will have been committed. Exceptions may be made in cases of accidental damage or when the works were urgently needed in the interests of health and safety. In these cases the Secretary of State must be informed as soon as reasonably practicable. It is necessary to seek the advice of English Heritage prior to carrying out any such work.

Current research and thought on medieval bridges

The arch is a stable structure, and the life of an arch bridge might be expected to be many times that of any other type. It is very rare indeed, although not unknown, for an arch bridge to fail due to the weight of the traffic passing across it. Arches can sustain loads of great weight, frequency and speed without marked change in their stability. Many medieval bridges are still capable of carrying concentrated loads of a size unimagined by their builders (figure 32). The National Bridge Assessment and Strengthening Programme has established that many historic bridges have an ultimate load-bearing capacity significantly in excess of their presumed capacity. Some bridges have unexpected structural features, such as internal spandrel walls, which contribute to

32. Trotton bridge, West Sussex, showing the scale of modern traffic.

this additional structural strength.

Such information was not available to engineers during the earlier twentieth century. Faced with undeniably clear signs of movement in ancient arches, they sought to secure them by the use of reinforced concrete, then called ferro-concrete. Many medieval and early post-medieval bridges were provided with a 'saddle' above their arches to remove the load from them. This was sometimes done without first clearly determining the reasons for the initial deterioration. A common reason for the movement of an arch is the spreading of the abutments on which it sits. If the distance between an arch's abutments increases by spreading, the only way that the arch can accommodate itself to the greater span is by allowing groups of its voussoirs to rotate, forming 'hinges'. Gaps may appear between voussoirs in the arch ring (figure 33), and the arch's shape can become visibly deformed. This can cause alarm; however, a 'three-hinge' arch is a well-known and completely safe structural form. Indeed, in practice an arch will never fit exactly between its abutments, and the 'cracked' state might be thought of as

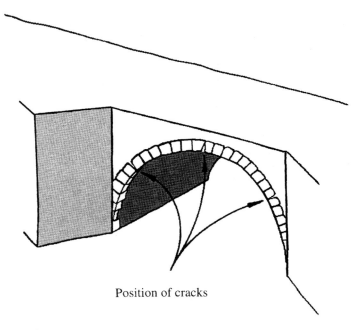

Position of cracks

33. Schematic drawing of an arch, showing the manner in which groups of voussoirs can rotate to produce a 'three-hinge' arch and, secondly, the position of cracks.

its natural condition. It is only with the appearance of a fourth hinge that the arch becomes unstable. The additional load of a concrete saddle, combined with the raising of the line of thrust which usually accompanies such a saddle, may increase the movement of the abutments, provoking the formation of a fourth hinge.

A common reason for the movement of a bridge's abutments is the erosion of the foundations. In 1986 in County Wicklow, Republic of Ireland, nine masonry bridges collapsed after a period of heavy rain. The subsequent 'bridge collapse seminar' in 1987, organised by An Foras Forbartha (the Republic of Ireland's national institute for physical planning and construction research), found that in eight of these cases the cause of failure was undermining of the foundations by a process known as 'scour'. In some cases river-bed levels had been lowered by up to 600 mm (2 feet) in situations where the foundations of the piers were only 300 mm (1 foot) deep. Shallow foundations are a common feature of English medieval bridges. However, it should not be thought that the use of shallow foundations was a defective technique. As has been noted above (in chapter 2) the medieval mason was a skilled workman, and this was a well-tried and proven construction method.

Scour occurs when obstructions, such as bridge abutments and piers, interfere significantly with the natural flow of a river. The effect is particularly pronounced when a pier lies oblique to the flow of the water. On meeting a pier the flow does not remain parallel to the bed of the river but dives down the pier's face creating a vortex (figure 34) which quarries a tear-drop shaped hole adjacent to the pier. It has been found that rounded piers are better than rectangular piers for reducing scour and that pointed piers are better than either. However, if debris is allowed to build up in front of a pier or if the course of the river changes, the pier's shape can be rendered irrelevant.

The usual means of counteracting these effects is to construct an apron of cobbles, rock fragments or concrete around the piers and abutments. Such an apron should be laid below the general scour level

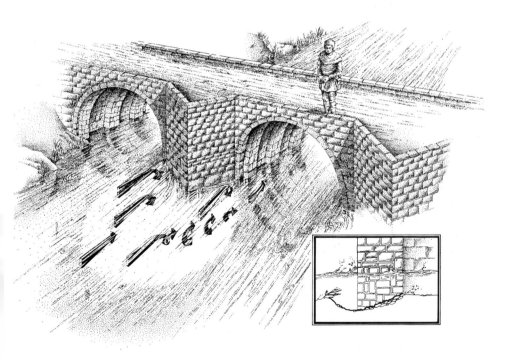

34. Schematic drawing of a bridge, showing the flow of water adjacent to a pier and the pattern of erosion that this can produce when scouring occurs.

35. Otley bridge, West Yorkshire, widened with reinforced concrete cantilevers.

of the river. However, research at the University of East Anglia has suggested an alternative solution. The construction of 'sacrificial piers' upstream of the bridge can relocate scour away from the bridge. This may be a useful alternative when original features (such as remains of piling or cobbled aprons) are known to exist in the bed of the river.

Usually it was not the need to carry additional loads that led to modifications or a replacement bridge but the demand for extra width as the quantity and speed of traffic increased. Bridges have been widened by erecting arches between adjacent pairs of cutwaters (figure 21), by cantilevering out on one or both sides (figure 35) or by building another structure alongside the original bridge. Each of these has its own advantages and disadvantages.

Widening a bridge by the construction of additional arches between adjacent pairs of cutwaters was the method of choice until recent times. Many ancient bridges have been widened in this manner. The advantage of the technique was that similar materials to those already in service were employed in an identical form of construction. Major rebuilding work did not have to be carried out, and the cost was therefore comparatively low. A disadvantage was that the pedestrian refuges were decreased in size, sometimes to the point when they were scarcely of any value (figure 36). On the approaches to a bridge, a related feature, the 'squinch arch' (figure 37) was employed to enable the parapets to be splayed into a funnel shape to assist the passage of vehicles approaching the bridge.

The use of cantilevers on one or both sides of a bridge is a solution of the twentieth century. This often goes hand-in-hand with complete replacement of the carriageway. The advantages of this technique are that the existing substructure is not significantly altered, provided that the foundations are capable of taking the extra load. Although the elevations of the bridge are substantially unaffected, they do tend to be lost to view beneath the shadow of the modern work. The use of materials with different engineering characteristics may also present difficulties. An arch constructed with stone blocks and mortar joints has a quite different response to changes in load, temperature and other factors from that of a reinforced concrete slab. A possible solution is to separate

36. Harrold Bridge, Bedfordshire, showing vestiges of pedestrian refuges that have been absorbed into the carriageway during the widening of the bridge.

37. Ludlow bridge, Shropshire. The approach to the bridge has been widened into a funnel with a 'squinch arch' to assist approaching traffic.

the different forms of construction with a thin membrane, enabling them to act independently.

The remaining solution is for the widening to be entirely independent of the former structure. This can be accomplished by building immediately alongside the existing bridge, or by the construction of an independent bridge a short distance up or down stream. The first option is the most challenging from an engineering point of view. It requires that the two structures be joined in such a way that differential settlement cannot occur and water cannot penetrate where they join. The problems associated with the juxtaposition of ancient and modern materials, of widely different engineering properties acting together, must also be addressed. The second option, that of constructing an entirely independent bridge nearby, generates two different problems. Firstly there is the possibility that changes to the river to accommodate a new bridge may alter the pattern of erosion at the existing one. Secondly, there is the issue of the bridge's place in the historic landscape, referred to as its 'setting'.

Planning Policy Guidance Note 16 states that the setting of an ancient monument is now a material consideration in determining a planning application, whether that monument is scheduled or not. The spirit of this guidance has been taken up in the *Design Manual for Roads and Bridges*, commonly known as the 'good roads guide'. In the section relating to heritage this states that 'the setting, not only of individual buildings, but also of archaeological monuments, historic towns and villages and landscape features is an essential part of their significance'. It adds that 'the integration of historic features with the road corridor can be important in reducing the impact of a road' and that `the re-use of historic bridges allows important structures to be kept, gives character to the road and can be cost-effective'. Clearly, if the capacity of a bridge is to be increased, the alterations must be sympathetically designed in order not to be intrusive.

A serious problem with historic masonry bridges is that their parapets are no longer adequate to meet present-day requirements. This is usually because they are insufficiently strong to restrain vehicles that have run out of control. Modern bridge parapets or railings have to be capable of containing and safely redirecting a medium to large saloon car travelling at 70 mph (113 km/h) and hitting the barrier at an angle of up to twenty degrees. An additional difficulty is presented by parapets that are now considered to be too low to protect pedestrians or cyclists from falling from the bridge. Packhorse bridges are an obvious example of the latter problem, and causeways may have no parapet at all, although a railing will frequently have been added by a cautious highway authority (figure 18).

Another major difficulty with ancient bridges is preventing water from entering the material lying between the top of the arches and the road. This often consists of whatever material was to hand when the bridge was built. It may have a high strength as a result of centuries of compaction and be contributing significantly to the stiffness of the bridge. However, the ingress of water, particularly in winter when it may be laden with salt, spread on the road in icy conditions, may result in crystallisation of the salt on the elevation or underside of the bridge. This can cause flaking and deterioration of the stone. Additionally, percolating water can cause washing-out of the finer components of the material, leaving voids. These can result in localised collapse of the road surface and potholes forming; the vibration caused when a vehicle hits a pothole can cause severe damage to the bridge. Further damage can occur if the material becomes saturated. This increases lateral pressure on the spandrel walls, which can be forced outwards. The effect is exacerbated if the saturated material freezes in winter.

Some general principles of conservation are that the minimum amount of intervention should be employed when it is necessary to stabilise a structure and that any such intervention should be recognisable and reversible at a later date. With regard to a bridge, the road surface should be kept waterproof and in a sound condition, and the pointing between the stones, both above and below the water, should be maintained. In addition, serious degeneration can be prevented by the periodic replacement of individual stones that have become so badly weathered or damaged that their structural integrity has been compromised, combined with the removal of vegetation growing on the structure, so that the need for major reconstruction is avoided. Wherever possible, modern materials should be eschewed in favour of those current at the time the bridge was built. Applying these principles to ancient bridges ensures that their historical integrity can be maintained as far as possible.

5
Further reading

Local, regional and national surveys

Cossins, J.A. 'Ancient Bridges, Fords and Ferries', *Transactions of the Birmingham Archaeological Society*, XLII (1916), 1-16.

Boyer, M.N. *Medieval French Bridges*. Medieval Academy of America, Cambridge (Massachusetts), 1976.

Harrison, D.F. 'Bridges and Economic Development ', *Economic History Review*, XLV (1992), 240-61.

Henderson, C., and Coates, H. *Old Cornish Bridges and Streams*. Simpkin Marshall, London, 1928.

Henderson, C., and Jervoise, E. *Old Devon Bridges*. A. Wheaton & Company, Exeter, 1938.

Jervoise, E. *The Ancient Bridges of the South of England*. Architectural Press, 1930.

Jervoise, E. *The Ancient Bridges of the North of England*. Architectural Press, 1931.

Jervoise, E. *The Ancient Bridges of Mid and Eastern England*. Architectural Press, 1932.

Jervoise, E. *The Ancient Bridges of Wales and Western England*. Architectural Press, 1936.

Maré, E. de. *The Bridges of Britain*. Batsford, 1954.

Masschaele, J. 'Transport Costs in Medieval England', *Economic History Review*, XLVI (1993), 266-79.

O'Keeffe, P., and Simington, T. *Irish Stone Bridges*. Irish Academic Press, Dublin, 1991.

Salzman, L.F. *Building in England down to 1540*. Clarendon Press, 1952.

Simco, A., and McKeague, P. *Bridges of Bedfordshire*. Bedfordshire County Council, 1997.

Thomas, D.L.B. 'The Chronology of Devon's Bridges', *Report and Transactions of the Devonshire Association*. 124 (1992), 175-206.

Studies of single bridges

Bourne, D. 'The Roman Bridge at Corbridge', *Archaeologia Aeliana*. XLV (1967), fourth series, 17-26.

Jackson, D.A., and Ambrose, T.M. 'A Roman Timber Bridge at Aldwinkle, Northamptonshire', *Britannia,* VII (1976), 39-72.

McKeague, P. 'Sutton Packhorse Bridge', *Bedfordshire Archaeology*, 18 (1988), 64-80.

Rowlands, M.L.J. *Monnow Bridge and Gate*. Alan Sutton, 1994.

Yates, N., and Gibson, J.M. (editors). *Traffic and Politics: The Construction and Management of Rochester Bridge AD 43-1993*. The Boydell Press, Woodbridge, 1994.

Technical writing

Alberti, L.B. *Ten Books on Architecture* (1485). Edited by J. Rykwert. Tiranti, 1955.

Davey, N. *Tests on Road Bridges*. National Building Studies, Research Paper number 16. HMSO, 1953.

Farraday, R.V., and Charlton, F.G. *Hydraulic Factors in Bridge Design*. Hydraulics Research, Wallingford, 1983.

Hammond, B.C. *Notes on the Strengthening of Two Historic Bridges in Worcestershire*. Paper presented to the West Midland Branch of the Institution of Municipal and County Engineers, Birmingham, November 1925.

Harvey, W.J. 'Assessment and Rehabilitation of Masonry Bridges', in *Bridge Rehabilitation* (167-77), edited by G. König and A.S. Nowak. Verlag für Architektur und technische Wissenschaften, Berlin, 1992.

Harvey, W.J., and Smith, F.W. 'Computer Aided Sketching of Load Paths: An Approach to the Analysis of Multi-span Arch Bridges', *Bridge Management,* edited by J.E. Harding and others. Spon, London, 1990.

Heyman, J. *The Masonry Arch*. Horwood, Chichester, 1982.

Lee, D. 'Comparative Maintenance Costs of Different Bridge Types', in *Bridge Management,* edited by J.E. Harding and others. Spon, London, 1990.

Page, J. (editor). *Masonry Arch Bridges*. Transport Research Laboratory, HMSO, 1993.

Paice, C. *Prevention of Local Scour at Bridge Piers*. Conference on the control of scour at bridge piers, University of East Anglia, Norwich, February 1992.

The medieval mason

Andrews, F.B. *The Medieval Builder and His Methods*. Oxford University Press, 1925.

Coldstream, N. *Masons and Sculptors.* British Museum Press, 1991; second impression 1993.

Harvey, J.H. *The Medieval Architect*. Weyland, London, 1972.

Knoop, D. *The Genesis of Freemasonry*. Manchester University Press, 1947.

Knoop, D., and Jones, G.P. 'Masons and Apprenticeship in Medieval England', *The Economic History Review*, III (1931), 346-66.

Knoop, D., and Jones, G.P. 'The Rise of the Mason Contractor', *Journal of the Royal Institute of British Architects*, October 1936, 1061-71.

Knoop, D., and Jones, G.P. 'The English Medieval Quarry', *Economic History Review*, IX (1938), 17-37.

Swanson, H. *Building Craftsmen in Late Medieval York*. Borthwick Institute of Historical Research, University of York, 1983.

6
Bridges to visit

The best view of a bridge is usually obtained from the fields on either side of it. Please remember that these may be private property and should be respected.

Large gorge bridges, of single or few arches
These are uncommon as they are dependent upon the geology being suitable for the formation of a gorge, within which such a bridge may be built.

> Framwelgate, County Durham (NZ 272424)
> Kirkby Lonsdale, Cumbria (SD 616782)
> Twizel, Northumberland (NT 884433)

Large, multiple-arch bridges
These are more common, spanning wide flood plains or estuaries, and may be found in many parts of Britain.

> Bakewell, Derbyshire (SK 219684)
> Bromham, Bedfordshire (TL 012506)
> Exeter, Devon (SX 915921)
> Great Barford, Bedfordshire (TL 135516)
> Harrold, Bedfordshire (SP 955565)
> Hereford, Herefordshire (SO 508396)
> Huntingdon, Cambridgeshire (TL 242714)
> Irthlingborough, Northamptonshire (SP 957706)
> Kildwick, West Yorkshire (SE 012457)
> Ludlow, Shropshire (SO 512742)
> Mordiford, Herefordshire (SO 569375)
> Newton Cap, County Durham (NZ 205302)
> Pershore, Worcestershire (SO 952452)
> St Ives, Cambridgeshire (TL 313712)
> Wadebridge, Cornwall (SW 991724)

Smaller medieval bridges
These were sometimes built over apparently insignificant streams, and one may come upon them unexpectedly. It is usually worth stopping to look. They are usually of two or three arches and often humpbacked in appearance.

> Alconbury, Cambridgeshire (TL 186757)
> Cringleford, Norfolk (TG 199059)
> Hadleigh, Suffolk (TM 025421)
> Spaldwick, Cambridgeshire (TL 126730)
> Trotton, West Sussex (SU 836223)
> Warcop, Cumbria (NY 743151)
> Yeolmbridge, Cornwall (SX 318873)

Fords

Fords on the public highway are now rarely found. The ease with which culverts can now be constructed on minor rivers and the dramatic changes in water level due to the development of inland navigation in the eighteenth century have resulted in the loss of these once common features. However, they often survive adjacent to packhorse bridges. Elsewhere, the approach to a former ford can usually be inferred from the widening of the highway near to a bridge.

Existing fords

Sutton, Bedfordshire (TL 220474)
Moulton, Suffolk (TL 697645)
Westerdale, North Yorkshire (NZ 662061)

Former fords

Alconbury Weston, Cambridgeshire (TL 176770)
Hamerton, Cambridgeshire (TL 136797)
Harrold, Bedfordshire (SP 955565)
Spaldwick, Cambridgeshire (TL 126730)

Packhorse bridges

These bridges are amongst the few visible relics of a once common method of transport. Because of their narrowness, they have often been replaced or buried during road-widening schemes.

Bishop's Itchington, Warwickshire (SP 404556)
Fifehead Neville, Dorset (ST 771114)
Gomshall, Surrey (TQ 084479)
Hebden Bridge, West Yorkshire (SD 992272)
Launceston, Cornwall (SX 328851)
South Church, County Durham (NZ 210284)
Sutton, Bedfordshire (TL 220474)
Utterby, Lincolnshire (TF 306932)
West Rasen, Lincolnshire (TF 063893)

Clapper bridges

The moors of Devon and Lancashire and the fells of Cumbria are famous for their clapper bridges, the dating of which is, at best, controversial.

Dartmeet, Devon (SX 672733)
Postbridge, Devon (SX 645789)
Wycoller, Lancashire (SD 932395)

Bridge chapels

All chapels, including those on or associated with bridges, suffered badly during the Reformation. Only two examples are known to survive, one of which is a reconstruction, although the sites of many are known through documentary sources.

Surviving examples
> St Ives, Cambridgeshire (TL 313712)
> Wakefield, West Yorkshire (SE 338201)

Documentary sources
> Exeter, Devon (SX 915921)
> Huntingdon, Cambridgeshire (TL 242714)
> Ludlow, Shropshire (SO 512742)
> Turvey, Bedfordshire (SP 938524)
> Wadebridge, Cornwall (SW 991724)

Fortified bridges and gatehouses
Most of these disappeared with the expansion of towns and the huge increase in the amount of traffic, particularly during the twentieth century. Only two examples of fortifications are known to have survived, one in fragmentary condition.

Surviving examples
> Monmouth, (SO 504125)
> Warkworth, Northumberland (NU 248062)

Documentary sources
> Morpeth, Northumberland (NZ 200858)
> Newton Cap, County Durham (NZ 205302)
> Hereford, Herefordshire (SO 508396)

Index